The Key Leadership Qualities It Takes to Be a BOSS... A Woman Entrepreneur in Business Today

How You Can Apply Leadership Principles and Use Them to Become an Entrepreneur

Book 1 – Women Entrepreneurs Series

by Judith LeComte Baker of LeBaker Music

www.LeBakerMusic.com

◆◆◆

Published by:
Judith LeComte Baker of LeBaker Music 2020

Cover Design by Shane Almgren

ISBN: 9798629445074

DEDICATION

This book is dedicated to my grandmother, the late Ollie Mae (Reed) Andrews. She taught and showed me by her example, that I CAN DO ANYTHING!

The life of poverty as a cotton cropper, in the mid-20th Century was not her idea of success. She escaped the clutches of the deep-south when my mother was only twelve years old. My Grandparents along with their large family, moved to the North to start a new life.

With barely a third-grade education, she taught herself a marketable but unique skill. "Ms. Ann," as she was often referred to, mastered that skill and created a thriving business that was well respected in the community. As a business owner and "entrepreneur" before society created a label for this role, she became a property owner and advocate for anyone oppressed.

She would often tell me "child you have to raise your own flag." Now, she was not referring to the white flag of surrender, but the flag of victory when a battle is won, so I did. I would not be where I am today had it not been for her faith in God, her influence, her guidance, her unconditional love and her thumb in my back.

CONTENTS

Introduction 1

Chapter One - So You Wanna Be Boss 3

Chapter Two - Kick-Start Your Entrepreneur Business 8

Chapter Three - The Key to Modern Leadership......................14

Chapter Four - Vital Lessons From Women of the Past 21

Chapter Five - Breaking Down Barriers....................................31

Chapter Six - The Right Mindset as a Woman Entrepreneur ...41

Chapter Seven - Making it as an Entrepreneur.........................45

Conclusion and Choices..52

About the Author 54

INTRODUCTION

When the urge of entrepreneurship calls you from deep within, it is a very hard signal to ignore. First, you start thinking about your concept incessantly. Then, it can start to feel like your current job, business, or life path is less interesting by the day. The idea to create your vision brews strong in your head, and it starts to feel like your only option is to make your idea a reality.

But what happens if you feel entirely sideswiped and knocked off your path? What if your best friend discourages you from pursuing your big idea and tells you to play it safe? What if the people you trust the most plant doubt in your mind?

If you are a woman reading this, you may be in the conception phase of your dream or pushing through the waves of questioning can my existing dream succeed. I know how fragile an idea can feel. Furthermore, I know the frustration of feeling like nobody has your back and maybe you should just stick to a nine-to-five job.

Whether you are starting or running your dream business such as: a health practice, selling your art collection, owning a coffee shop, creating an app, or pursuing a freelance consulting career, this book will show you that it is all possible as long as you never ever give up.

Whatever dream you are ready to bring to life or have already birthed, this book will serve as a fountain of wisdom and knowledge to help you withstand the challenging stages of business as an entrepreneur.

I want you to find comfort in knowing that you are not the only one who has questioned your entire sanity, decision making capabilities and self-worth as a woman, while following your passion, a dream many people in your life may not buy into or at least, not yet understand.

"We need to accept that we won't always make the right decisions, that we'll screw up royally sometimes – understanding that failure is not the opposite of success, it's part of success." - Arianna Huffington

If you are reading this book, then you are already a woman who has taken a huge leap of faith. You are on your path of entrepreneurship for the long run. Only you can write the pages of your own story. Enjoy the journey and learn from this book. Lean from the truth and insight provided particularly just for you. I hope that you read these pages and take the nuggets to heart to become even stronger!

The book contains the following discussions in detail:

- The Businesswoman
- Kick-Start That Business
- The Key to Modern Female Leadership
- Vital Lessons from Women of the Past
- Breaking Gender Barriers Down
- Real-Life Case Study – James
- Conclusion and Choices

Thank you for selecting this book. May it be a life-changing boost to you as you endeavor to be the woman entrepreneur of your dream.

CHAPTER ONE – SO YOU WANNA BE BOSS

"The destiny of the woman must be shaped to a large extent on her own conception of her spiritual imperative and her place in society." - Sandra Day O'Connor

When I made the decision to start my own business, I was excited about the potential to make an impact. Finally, I could do things in my own way, rather than being a cog in the corporate world fattening someone else's bank account. I could help people I really wanted to help. I could have the money to give to charities I am passionate about. I could enjoy the time and freedom for the events and activities my family and I dream about. I enjoy helping others, and that is honestly my primary reason for writing this book - helping other women, who are entrepreneurial spirits like me, is very exhilarating.

In our family, starting something new is always an adventure. I remember participating in my first 5K race. It was a beautiful sunny day in Albuquerque, New Mexico, and I had been looking forward to this day for weeks. It was early fall; the weather was perfect, and the race would raise funding for the local Zoo. Even before the starting gun, I was already visualizing crossing the finish line, victorious. I just knew that I would proudly stand in the winner's circle with that beautiful, blue 1st place ribbon hanging around my neck. After all, at the time I was serving in the military. I had trained long, hard, and well.

If only it was that easy. The people I thought I would leave in a trail of dust were much faster than I anticipated. They were tougher competition than I was prepared for. As I ran, my energy started to perish, and that finish line looked far away. I didn't finish first that day. But I did finish, and I'm proud of the effort I made.

Starting a business is clearly more challenging than a one-time race but, it is a good parallel to contrast against. I tend to think of the ebbs and flows of business as hurdles. Imagine if this 5k I ran had hurdles. I would encounter those hurdles as more challenges in addition to my competition and I would probably experience painful setbacks. I would ask myself: What if the hurdle is too high and there's no way to jump over it? What happens if I don't properly train and assume, I can clear the hurdles?

In business we need to prepare and plan for overcoming hurdles. Unlike a race, being successful in business can be about collaboration rather than competition. There is enough market for anyone willing to put the effort into their dream.

In contrast, when we run a race, the rules are clear. We wait for the starting gun to fire. We stay on the track. We know the running pace we need to complete the race. We can even prepare for the hurdles. None of these givens are evident in business. There isn't one set off rules available for anyone to follow that guarantees you will reach the finish line. Furthermore, there isn't a finish line or even milestones unless we have defined them for ourselves.

One common milestone that many business owners aspire to is to make six figures of revenue from their business. Another goal may be to replace the income from a day job. As with anything worthwhile in life, you must put in the effort and work hard. You must be committed. But you can create a plan that puts your racetrack and finish line clearly in your sight.

Ready? Let's look at the three common mistakes entrepreneurs often make in the beginning stages of starting their business.

Reason 1: You Don't Know Your Numbers and You Don't Have a Plan

If you are like most women entrepreneurs that I know, you love your business. Your challenge is you can't figure out how to consistently make the money you want every month. Let's look at this example with Mary Beth.

When Mary Beth came to me, she had this problem. She was short about $3,000 a month in revenue to cover all her expenses, including her living expenses. Even though her appointment book was full every day, she didn't have any more time in her day to take on more clients. Mary Beth was already working at her full capacity.

When I started working with her, I found that Mary Beth didn't have some of the basic business structures in place which she needed to be successful. She had about 100 clients, however, she didn't have an actual client list. Also, Mary Beth was not regularly recording and tracking her sales numbers. For example, in preparation for her taxes, every January, she would go through her appointment book, write down all the prices she had charged each of her clients, and then add them up with a calculator to give to her accountant. Can you imagine how much time that took her? And, she had no idea how much her business did in revenue from month to month. She lacked insight into where in her business is the greatest return on her investment based on her present business model.

Successful business owners know their numbers. They know how much revenue each of their services or programs are bringing in monthly. They know details, such as is their revenue impacted by seasons. For example, is December a great month or a slow month? They know how many clients they have and market to them regularly.

Additionally, successful business owners have a business plan. This is the roadmap to their business success. Having a business plan is like having a racetrack clearly in front of you that you can now follow to achieve your business goals. There are many free resources available online and in metropolitan communities that can help craft a solid business plan. One option is to find a fellow sister entrepreneur that may be willing to barter services for some business planning and advise. If you're good with internet research, do a Google search for "business plans." Don't rule out the small business administration at sba.gov. All of the components of a business plan will be presented in a future book in this series.

Reason 2: Focusing on the Wrong Activities

Over a century ago, Vilfredo Pareto was surprised to find that 20% of the peapods in his garden contained 80% of the peas. Based on this and on a finding that 80% of the land in Italy was owned by 20% of the population, Pareto developed the Pareto Principle, which many of us know as the 80/20 rule. The 80/20 rule holds in many situations, particularly in business. In most cases, 80% of your revenue comes from 20% of your clients. Just think about that for a moment- 20% of your clients pay your bills.

The 80/20 rule also applies to your daily activities. If you are like most business owners, only 20% of your activities are relevant to the success of your business. The key takeaways to contemplate are:

- What opportunity is there in the other 80% of your activities and clients?
- What percentage of your daily activities is directly impacting your revenue?

For example, when Mary Beth came to me, she knew she had gaps in her business. Her main problem was that she was not making enough money to meet her monthly obligations. As a first step, I asked her to write down her daily activities, hour by hour, for five straight days.

What we found was Mary Beth was spending 80% of her time seeing clients and very little time on sales and marketing. Her remaining 20% was focused on administrative tasks. When we talked about refocusing her daily activities, I saw a light bulb ignite in Mary Beth's eyes. Together, we made a sales and marketing plan to support her business, and we defined her daily activities to support increasing her revenue.

One thing we did was use her e-mail list to automate marketing to her clients. With today's technology and several free email-marketing tools, this is a relatively simple and often a one-time process. Mary Beth imported the Excel file containing her client list into a service. She then scheduled e-mails to go out on a regular basis leaving her free to focus on other business-related activities. As part of her e-mail campaigns, Mary Beth scheduled announcements for promotional events and sent personalized messages to honor the special days in the lives of her clients, all from an automated e-mail marketing system.

Next, we looked for ways she could replicate herself. Some of her services were training. She created on-line classes for clients to access her material for a fee, creating another stream of income. This expanded her business globally without the need for Mary Beth to physically teach in a traditional classroom.

Every quarter, we went back and revisited her plan. Monthly, using a spreadsheet, Mary Beth calculated the return on her investment. She could see her growth per month, and she could see where adjustments needed to be made to her business model - a much better method of forecasting for her business.

Reason 3: Your Pricing is Broken

While Mary Beth had all the clients she needed, we needed to take a closer look at her pricing. I showed her several new pricing scenarios and compared those to the revenue her current pricing was generating. The difference was eye-opening for her.

Then the real work started. What my sales forecast scenarios demonstrated in simple numbers was that she either needed to take on more clients or raise her prices. Because her schedule was already packed with clients, taking on more wasn't an option, so it was clear that she needed to raise her prices.

Mary Beth hadn't raised her prices in years, especially for her long-term loyal clients, and she had a real fear of asking for more money. I became the voice of reason for her gently helping her through her fear. We found other ways to reward the loyalty of her long-term clients. We grandfathered a small portion of her long-term, most loyal clients and set up a pricing scale more scalable and incremental. Mary Beth still has more work to do to make up the full $3,000, but she has made great progress, and I have no doubt that she will get there.

CHAPTER TWO – KICK-START YOUR ENTREPRENEUR BUSINESS

"Individuals need to be willing to face the truth about their attitudes, behaviors, even what we want out of life."
- Joyce Meyer

For most women, starting the business can seem like the hardest part of the process. So many times, we can get caught up in brainstorming and the planning. As women, we tend to be nurturing creatures and the temptation to protect our entrepreneurial baby can take over. When one ventures into uncharted territory impacting our livelihood, the natural instinct of fight or flight surfaces.

When that instinct is flight, you can quickly become stuck in a procrastination phase that is driven by an underlying fear of failure. Next, doubts and frustrations creep in and nothing progresses except ideas with no activity, re-written to-do lists, scenarios of things like ... what is my logo going to look like ... what if I can't do it, etc. It is time to ditch your fear-based procrastination by kick-starting your business out of flight mode and into fight mode.

This chapter will outline the exact steps you need to take to simply get started. If you are up and running, use this chapter to assess if there are any gaps in your existing business. Let's examine your entrepreneurial baby by looking at, the Product, the Launch, and, most importantly, the **SALES**!

The Product

Every business must provide one of two things: a product or a service. What is YOUR PRODUCT or WHAT SERVICE CAN YOU PROVIDE? The biggest hang up is the thinking "what can you provide that's missing from the market?" or "what service can you provide that isn't out there?" Here's a refreshing newsflash for you, your product or service doesn't have to be missing or undiscovered. It just needs to be GOOD. Your new business can even be - WHAT CAN I DO BETTER?

In this wonderful age of social media, EVERYONE has a product. In most cases, the product is rarely good, yet, it SELLS! This is where our focus starts. What product or service can you create that will SELL! Because, at the end of the day, sales are what pay the bills, not debating over logos or what if's! Trust me, if your product is good, your logo won't matter.

So, let's dive in. You have your product. Now, let's sell it. Again, I'm not here to talk hypotheticals. Get a pen and paper so you can take notes as your wheels start spinning. I'm going to tell you what you need to do to get your entrepreneurial dream up and running.

The Launch

In order to sell a product successfully, you need a website. There's really no way around this. The first thing I look for when I see a product, I like is their website. The second thing I check to see is whether I can buy the products I'm interested in from their website. CAN I ADD THIS TO MY CART AND CHECKOUT?!!! Not: can I fill out a form so you can contact me.

Did you know that it is very affordable to create a website? Most people don't know this, or the thought of technology is overwhelming. When I started my business, LeBaker Music, I did it all myself using a domain hosting service and WordPress.

Here are ten things you need to build an amazing website:

1. Your business name – you want to make sure that you have a catchy name for your business; be sure that it sounds professional
2. Your mission, vision, and background story – something that is meaningful and draws people in

3. Research – look at the websites of your competition and any websites you think fit your brand; on paper, create a mock-up of what you want on each page
4. Your product or service information, description, size, etc.
5. Great content for your website pages – Home page, Store page, About Us page, Contact Us page
6. Pictures of your products
7. What you want to call your website – your domain name; come up with 3-5 options just in case your first choice is taken
8. You will need to host your domain – I prefer Bluehost, but GoDaddy is a great option as well
9. Log in to WordPress and build your website – WordPress is free, and there are many free templates you can use; keep it simple
10. Integrate your merchant services – How are you going to sell your product? PayPal? Square? WooCommerce? This may even be the most important aspect of your site. Think about it, if you have a customers' attention, but they can't buy your product, they will move on.

The next step is to brand all of your content around your business name. For example, make sure your Instagram and Facebook business pages are in line with your brand - same logo, same name, same colors, and similar content. You want people to notice your content and products across the board.

The best way is to keep your business based social media in sync is to use a social media manager with scheduling features. Scheduling social media posts will keep you active and build your tribe, even when you are focused on the other aspects of your business. Lastly, don't be afraid to take advantage of social media. Do a test run of your product and introduce it to your friends on Facebook, just to test the market.

When I started, I had to figure this all out for myself. Now, if the whole technology step is what is holding you back, hire someone! You can find reasonable help on Fiverr.com and Upwork.com (a few freelance sites). There is also the techy nephew or niece that we all have that can knock this out in an hour. Get help where it makes sense!

The Sale

How do you price your product or service? There are a couple of ways to figure out a price that is right for your product. One way is to check what price products similar to yours are selling for. I have noticed many people look at other people's pricing and go lower. This may not be the best approach and you could be reducing the value of your product or service.

One major key to developing a successful brand is to BELIEVE THAT YOU ARE THE BEST AT WHAT YOU CREATE OR THE SERVICE THAT YOU PROVIDE, even if you aren't there just yet. We all know that practice makes it perfect. But, don't sell yourself short.

Successfully generating customers and repeat customers requires upfront pricing. Here is an example: many people have a sliding scale, depending on who you are and how much money they can get from you. That is not a best practice in business. Furthermore, this method is very difficult to manage. Remember, customers talk and word will get around that your pricing is not fair. You could lose customers or even find yourself in a lawsuit because someone perceived you as being discriminatory. As the saying goes, "Ain't nobody got time for that!"

Select your price and be firm. Be happy about the price you chose and stand by it. Trust me, your customers will appreciate your honesty. When potential customers google you, it is important for them to find not just your product but also the price. They will either buy your product or they won't. More than likely they will add it to the cart if your product is good. Just keep in mind that we often, if not always, spend money on the things we want!

EXTRA TIP: remember WordPress? Install a "cart reminder" plug-in to alert customers to check out after they leave your site.

Now, it is time to do a self-assessment. Grab that pad and paper, and let's see if you missed anything. By now you have accomplished a few things.

1. You decided on your product or service
2. You have named your baby – your website
3. You set up your website and your merchant services, such as PayPal
4. You have snapped pics and introduced your baby to the world, i.e., through social media
5. You are selling and making money

So, what's next?

Well, you may have a business, but right now you are a sole proprietorship. That means if you find yourself in a legal battle, your opponent can come after everything you own including your business.

Become an LLC (Limited Liability Company)

Now, this isn't something you need to do right away, but put it on your two-month plan. You want to initiate your business and sell your product a bit just to make sure it works for you. What's the point of an LLC or paying taxes on a business that isn't generating income? A LOT of people jump the gun here, and typically get stuck with an LLC or doing business as a company that doesn't go anywhere …. This is not what you're going to do!

When you're ready and your product is doing well in the market …. Creating an LLC is easy! Go online and get your free EIN (employer identification number) from the IRS at irs.gov. It literally takes two minutes, and you'll need this to complete your LLC paperwork.

You can literally do it right from your cell phone. Google your state's website and fill out the forms online. Depending on your state, it should cost about $200-$300. That's all, and the forms will be mailed to you in about three weeks with your registered LLC. With anything business related, make sure you seek the appropriate legal advice. Do your research and decide what works best for you.

Dominate Your Marketing!
Marketing is the direct voice of your product/service to your customer. It is how you introduce your product, how you sell your product and most importantly, how you engage with your buyers. Marketing tells the story of what you have, how it brings value, how it solves a problem and how people can enjoy it.

Marketing success, using video is a powerful tool. Success does not come using some random video, but videos should catch a customer's attention both visually and acoustically. Videos need to make people feel something emotive, usually positive. Music is a great way to accomplish a connection to your customer in a video.

Think about when you hear a song and it takes you back to a happy moment from your past? Look at television commercials and the style of music playing in the background. You are most likely to hear songs that are upbeat, fun and evoke a happy feeling. Commercials featuring smiles, laughter, great-times and overcoming health issues are all backed by this style of soundtrack. Use this same advertising technique in your product videos.

It's very important to keep your content fresh and engaging. Think of marketing as your creative outlet. This is the socially engaging part that welcomes the world to your business.

If you have actually started your business and I hope you have by now, welcome to the Entrepreneurs life. Celebrate and tell yourself **CONGRATULATIONS!**

I like to reward myself for reaching my business milestones, so do something nice and inexpensive to enjoy the moment of success! Take a hot bath, spend some time cooking, read your favorite magazine, do your nails or spend the day outside. It doesn't have to be something expensive or unhealthy. You are just getting started so save your resources and let's not add any unhealthy extra pounds from overindulgence.

Next, come back to reality and do yourself a huge favor - remember, in order to be great, you must work harder than ever before! But - YOU CAN DO IT!

CHAPTER THREE - THE KEY TO MODERN LEADERSHIP

It's about knowing yourself and what you're good at. Females, males – anyone can be anything they want to be."
- Payal Kadakia

Leadership encompasses numerous ideas and values. The dictionary definition is the action of leading a group of people or an organization. However, real leadership goes way beyond this simple definition. Often, what it means to lead is subject to interpretation and jaded by various personality types.

Effective leadership embodies a combination of different leadership styles which are applied in an appropriate and timely manner. In this chapter, we will examine leadership from a business perspective, examine the different styles of leadership and identify when they are appropriate. After all, we as entrepreneurs are business leaders.

In a corporate environment, leadership depends on senior managers in the organization, to set challenging goals, inspire and motivate people to achieve those goals. Senior managers embody and evangelize the company's vision and values as the means to motivate and inspire employees to perform. Together leadership drives the performance of the business to the highest level possible.

Leadership as an entrepreneur is no different. You will need to do the same activities as the leaders in the business world. You will interact with some of them and they will be your customer. It is important to understand leadership and how to set challenging goals for your own business. Once you have employees, how will you inspire and motivate your people to achieve these goals.

When a business performs well, hits targets, and is level with or ahead of its competitors, this is due to good leadership. Poor performance correspondingly is usually a result of poor leadership. Therefore, you will often see a change in leadership shortly after a business announces poor performance figures. Leadership sets the direction that a company is headed in and then steers it towards that direction.

Awesome Female Leadership

Meg Whitman joined eBay in 1998, as CEO. At that time, the company employed a total of 30 people and grossed $4,000,000 a year. By the end of 2008, under Whitman's leadership, the company had grown beyond all expectations, employed 15,000 people and grossed$8,000,000,000. Ms. Whitman stepped down as CEO that same year, but her legacy as an incredibly effective leader is indisputable. 2008 was also the year that she was inducted into the U.S. Business Hall of Fame.

So, what was it about Meg Whitman's leadership that brought eBay from a quirky, mildly successful business to a multi-billion-dollar powerhouse? Whitman gave the business some much-needed direction through her leadership. She was passionate about putting customers first and transforming eBay's website from "clunky" and difficult to use, to slick and user-friendly. She reorganized the company, splitting it into twenty-three different business categories and appointing executives to lead each category. She was determined to set a clear vision and to make sure that everyone in the company understood the vision as well as their part to play in achieving it. She knew that for eBay to reach the success she envisioned; she would need to have everybody on board.

To do this, Whitman also focused on employee engagement, believing that the best results come from a motivated and happy workforce. Her employees have been known to describe her as "relentlessly optimistic" and how they admired her ability to stay focused and positive. As a result of Whitman's leadership style, employees were more empowered, the business functioned more efficiently, and customer satisfaction increased dramatically - not to mention, of course, the profits!

Leadership Styles

All business leaders are mostly aiming for the same outcome of high profit and a stable business that can withstand unpredictable outside forces. However, the way they approach it can differ significantly. There are numerous leadership styles and various models that explore the different ways people approach leadership. It would take an entirely new book to cover them all. So, for the purposes of this chapter, we'll look at a couple of the most common and influential leadership style models.

As you read these leadership styles, think about which one you admire the most, what is your leadership style, which leadership style do you prefer, and most importantly, which leadership style(s) do you need to embrace and further develop to take your business to the highest level.

Lewin's Leadership Styles

One of the earliest studies of leadership styles was led by psychologist Kurt Lewin in 1939. Lewin and his team identified three core leadership styles that formed a basis for later, more complex leadership theories. The study involved assigning three groups of schoolchildren to be led by one of the three types of leader: autocratic, democratic, or laissez-faire. The researchers then noted the children's response and performance under the different types of leadership.

These three types of leadership are a common model used in leadership and management courses across the globe. Let's take a closer look at how the three different styles compare:

1. Autocratic Leadership

Autocratic leaders are authoritarian meaning; they hold the entire concentration of power and expect submission to their authority. They set clear expectations and timelines. In this leadership style, the leader makes all decisions independently, without seeking any input from their followers. Autocratic leadership sets a clear divide between the leader and the followers.

The positives of this style are that employees are given clear instructions and understand what is expected of them. It's useful in situations where deviation from rules and standards can have dramatic consequences. For example, it may be the style of leadership most appropriate to a heavily regulated industry or a military combat mission.

The negatives are that it discourages creative thinking, it breeds poor employee engagement, and it can be seen as a very dictatorial style. Autocratic leadership can create a very hostile environment when used inappropriately leading to an "us and them" mentality, where employees and leaders appear to be on opposite sides.

Autocratic leadership is generally considered quite an old-fashioned style of leadership that has more limitations than positives. It's a helpful style to adopt in certain situations that need a strong leader to take charge and make decisions, but it's rarely an appropriate style to use every day.

2. Democratic Leadership

Democratic leaders encourage group participation in activities and two-way discussions. They will often provide guidance and advice but are less likely to provide rigid rules and instructions. They generally value the outcome over the process. Democratic leaders encourage followers to voice their opinions on decisions, but they retain the final say. By encouraging participation, democratic leaders foster better engagement and more motivated followers. It also allows for more creative thinking and more effective teamwork.

In Lewin's study, this was the most effective leadership style. Although the children in this group produced less than the children in the autocratic group, the output was of a higher quality.

3. Laissez-Faire Leadership

Laissez-faire leaders provide very little direction or guidance and encourage followers to make decisions themselves with little or no input from the leader. In Lewin's study, this group produced the least and had the most trouble both cooperating and working independently. They were also the most demanding of the leader.

Newer Leadership Styles and Models

Those three leadership styles are fairly polarizing, and few leaders fit neatly into those categories all of the time. However, Lewin's work provided a foundation for other studies into leadership theory that has expanded and developed into a variety of leadership styles. Here are some of the more popular leadership styles that have been identified.

1. Transactional Leadership

Transactional leadership is most closely related to Lewin's autocratic leadership style. In this leadership style, the relationship between leader and follower is completely transactional and usually based on financial compensation for tasks completed.

The transactional leader gives clear instructions and sets expectations. Followers are clear on what is expected of them, and what the expected compensation will be. Transactional leaders may offer incentives for high performance as a motivational tool, but they don't tend to recognize employee engagement as necessary or relevant to their organization.

Like autocratic leadership, this leadership style tends to result in less creative thinking. It's a suitable style for leaders in positions where their employees are producing high volumes like in manufacturing, or in high volume sales. It is least suitable for leaders who need their employees to solve complex problems or come up with creative solutions regularly.

2. Situational Leadership

Situational leadership is a leadership model that encompasses different styles. The basis of this model is that while there are different styles, they should vary by situation and not by the individual. It recognizes that different leadership challenges need different leadership approaches. One of the most popular models of situational leadership is the Hersey-Blanchard Model that identifies four core leadership styles:

Telling - Much like the autocratic style, this is where the leader gives directions and expects the employees to follow without many questions.

Selling - This is where the leader recognizes the need to persuade employees or followers to buy into an idea or vision.

Participating -This is where the leader encourages employees or followers to have an active role in decision making, but the leader remains hands-on and involved.

Delegating - This is like the laissez-faire style, where a leader steps back and allows the group a lot of autonomy over decisions.

The key to this model is that none of these styles are considered superior. They are all better suited to different situations, and a good leader will be able to identify and employ the appropriate style for any given situation.

In this model, the style a leader chooses will depend in part on the "maturity" level of the employees, along with the task itself. Their maturity level is their knowledge and competence in the role. For employees with low knowledge and competence, a delegating style would be inappropriate for most tasks, as those employees would need a high level of guidance and supervision. For highly skilled and competent employees, one of the more hands-off approaches would be suitable in most cases.

3. Transformational Leadership

Transformational leadership is a leadership style that is generally considered to be one of the most effective. Transformational leaders are excellent at motivating and inspiring followers to achieve goals. They are usually energetic and passionate speakers with high emotional intelligence. They value the individual contributions of their followers and readily offer praise and recognition. Transformational leaders often take on a coaching and mentoring role with their employees. They want to support and develop the people they lead, nurturing their talents and placing people in positions that suit their unique strengths.

> This style is particularly well-suited to identifying how an organization needs to change and leading them through that change. Considering the fast pace of most industries in this day and age, the ability to lead change effectively is an essential skill for anyone aspiring to be an entrepreneur.

In several studies, this style of leadership has been shown to drive higher staff engagement and higher performance than other styles. Meg Whitman is one example of a leader who embodied a transformational leadership style. Studies have shown that women naturally tend to have a transformational leadership style. Leadership researcher Bernard Bass conducted one of the studies which concluded that women tend to have more characteristics aligned with transformational leadership.

Leadership theory is a thriving subject, and these leadership styles barely scratch the surface of the complex study of leadership. They do, however, provide a good basis for understanding some of the more common styles of leadership.

ACTION ITEM FOR YOU - what do you need to change or deeper develop with your own leaderships style?

CHAPTER FOUR – VITAL LESSONS FROM WOMEN OF THE PAST

"I think the truth of the matter is, people who end up as 'first' don't actually set out to be first. They set out to do something they love and it just so happens that they are the first to do it."
- Former Secretary of State Condoleezza Rice

Although female leadership, on the scale we know it today, is fairly new. There have been examples of women in leadership positions all throughout history. Women have led nations, founded religious organizations, built businesses, and led social movements. And, for most of history, they have done so against incredible odds.

Let's take a look at some of the most notable examples of historical women in leadership and what we can learn from them.

Cleopatra

Cleopatra is arguably one of the most famous women in leadership of all time. Her infamous affairs with Roman leaders Julius Caesar and then later, Mark Antony sometimes overshadow her achievements as the last Pharaoh of Ptolemaic Egypt. Her father was King Ptolemy XII. After his death, the throne passed to Cleopatra and her ten-year-old brother, Ptolemy XIII. Cleopatra was 18 at the time. During this time, Egypt suffered from a poor economy and political turmoil.

Shortly after they ascended the throne, a rift began to appear between Cleopatra and her brother. The differences between them led to Cleopatra fleeing to Syria in order to assemble an army to take back the throne. Eventually, it was a romantic alliance with Julius Caesar that saw Ptolemy XIII defeated and Cleopatra restored to the throne as queen. After Caesar's death, Cleopatra was summoned to Rome by Mark Antony, beginning her second affair with a Roman politician. Cleopatra ruled Egypt for around two decades, but there are few records of her achievements as a ruler. Most historical accounts concentrate on her influence over Roman politicians and not her own country.

It's said, and Hollywood has certainly repeated the story in film, that Mark Antony killed himself after being defeated by his rival Octavian and believing Cleopatra to be dead. When Cleopatra discovered this, she is said to have committed suicide by being bitten by an asp. The location of her burial has never been discovered.

Queen Elizabeth I

Queen Elizabeth was the daughter of Henry VIII and Anne Boleyn. She ascended to the English throne in 1558, aged 25, after the death of her brother Edward VI. She remained on the throne until her death in 1603 and reigned over a period of great change and growth. She introduced the first form of welfare in England and famously defeated the Spanish Armada. Elizabeth was also responsible for building on her father's legacy and transforming England into a country of Protestant faith. Her tolerant approach that allowed Puritans and Catholics to continue following their faith earned her a lot of approval. She still faced threats from Catholics however, who wanted to see her Catholic cousin, Mary, on the throne.

Elizabeth was an intelligent queen with a lot of political savvy. However, she was not without her critics. During her reign, Parliament became more influential, and there was conflict over several issues, such as religion, her refusal to marry, and trade monopolies. Elizabeth's reign is seen as a "golden age" of English culture when Shakespeare was writing his plays and theatre became popular. To this day, the era of her reign is known as the " Elizabethan era."

Queen Victoria

Another English Queen, Victoria, reigned for 63 years and survived six potential assassination attempts. She was the first queen to rule from Buckingham Palace and was the longest-serving British monarch until the reign of Elizabeth II. Victoria was queen during the rapid expansion of the British Empire, and she eventually ruled over the largest empire in history. During her reign, England experienced great advances in science, industry, communications and the building of railways.

Standing at only four-feet, eleven-inches, she was, for the most part, a Queen who promoted peace and tolerance. Under her rule, all British colonies abolished slavery. She married her first cousin, Prince Albert, of Saxe-Coburg and Gotha, the son of her mother's brother in 1840. Initially, Victoria ensured that Albert, a German, had no part in governing the country, but over time, as she bore nine children, she relented and allowed him a larger political role. It is said that Albert became her strongest supporter helping her make crucial decisions during difficult political times. The couple was very devoted to each other.

To quell the growing republican movement, Victoria ushered in a new era of a more visible monarchy. She became a patron of numerous charities and made hundreds of civic visits. After Albert's death, however, she withdrew from public life and spent the majority of her time at Balmoral. She did reemerge into the public eye later, and her golden and diamond jubilees were widely celebrated across the British Empire. The era of her reign is commonly referred to the "Victorian era."

Anna Bissell

In 1876, Melville Bissell invented a one-of a kind "sweeper" by accident. Tired of dealing with a sawdust mess in their crockery and china shop, located in Grand Rapids, Michigan, the new sweeper provided a more effective and efficient way to clean carpet. This invention caught the attention of friends, generated customers and the Bissell business was born.

In 1889, after the untimely death of Bissell, it was clear that his wife, Anna Bissell would take the leadership position. Anna already knew all aspects of the business from end to end. Anna became the very first female CEO in the United States. She ran the company from 1889 until 1919 and was the Chair of the Board from 1919-1934. By all accounts, she was an aggressive and innovate leader, bringing the

Bissell brand of carpet cleaners and vacuums to the international market.

Under her leadership, the company expanded into to a strong business and reportedly, even Queen Victoria insisted on there being a Bissell at Buckingham Palace. By 1899, Bissell was the largest organization of its kind.

Anna Bissell was the embodiment of a transformational leader, implementing labor policies like workman's-compensation and pension plans before these were the norm. She had a reputation of respect, admiration, fairness and genuine concern for people which garnered commitment and loyalty from her employees. Anna Sutherland Bissell died in 1943 and was acclaimed as "a successful businesswoman in an era where business was almost wholly a masculine field."

Eleanor Roosevelt

"No one can make you feel inferior without your consent."
- Eleanor Roosevelt

I think Eleanor Roosevelt said those words just for me and I sure grew up hearing them especially from the leading ladies in my family. My Aunt Lil' adored Eleanor Roosevelt. After completing the research for this book, I completely understand why. My aunt, a woman born in an era equally oppressive to minorities as well as her "delicate" gender, grew up watching and directly benefiting from the efforts and achievements of Ms. Roosevelt's. So just for Aunt Lil' I may have spent a little extra effort researching Lady Eleanor.

Eleanor Roosevelt was the first wife of a sitting president to take an active role in American politics. She started life as a shy and insecure child but overcame her low self-esteem and perceived awkwardness while attending London's Allenswood Academy. Her teacher Mademoiselle Marie Souvestre, a passionate woman who embraced social issues expanded Eleanor's affluent world view. During these formative years her social and political ideal were developed.

Up until President Roosevelt's election, the function of a first lady was purely social. However, Eleanor had been campaigning on her husband's behalf throughout his political career. She'd also established businesses of her own. She used a factory facility to help Hyde Park families supplement their income and she purchased a girl's school where she taught.

When her husband was elected, Eleanor was not content to sit back and attend social functions. Instead, she paved the way for future first ladies by holding press conferences, writing a newspaper column, authoring books and supporting civil and women's rights movements, among other activities. With the passage of women's suffrage in 1920, First Lady, Eleanor Roosevelt is the reason women in America can vote today.

Even after her husband's death, Eleanor continued to have political influence. She campaigned for presidents, including John F. Kennedy, was appointed as a United Nations delegate, and continued to support civil rights movements.

Indira Priyadarshini Gandhi

Indira Gandhi was the first female Prime Minister of India. She is also the second-longest serving prime minister. Gandhi served for several terms but was assassinated by her own bodyguards in October 1984. Her introduction to politics began when she served as her father's personal assistant during his time as prime minister. She was elected as president of the Indian National Congress. After her father's death, she joined the cabinet as minister of Information and Broadcasting. In 1966 she was elected as prime minister of India.

Gandhi took India to war with Pakistan in 1971, and, under her leadership, India's armed forces were victorious. That victory led to the creation of Bangladesh, and Gandhi was the first government leader to recognize the new country. After a challenge from the opposing party that could have banned her from politics for six years, Gandhi appealed to the Supreme Court. When their response was not what she anticipated, she declared a state of emergency throughout India. During this time, she assumed emergency powers, imprisoned her opponents, and passed several new laws. Many of her measures were highly unpopular and included a mass sterilization drive.

Emergency rule ended in 1977, and, along with it, Gandhi's tenure as prime minister. In 1980, however, she was re-elected as prime minister once more and served until her assassination. Her final term was filled with controversy, predominantly over the handling of escalating conflicts with Sikh separatists.

Barbara Jordan

Barbara Jordan, a member of the U.S. House of Representatives, became both the first woman and the first African American to deliver a keynote speech at the 1976 Democratic National Convention.

> "We are a people in a quandary about the present. We are a people in search of our future. We are people in search of a national community. We are a people trying not only to solve the problems of the present, but we are attempting on a larger scale to fulfill the promise of America." - Barbara Jordan, July 12, 1976

After hearing a career-day speech delivered by attorney Edith S. Sampson, in the segregated Texas high school Jordan attended, she was inspired to become an attorney. She earned her undergraduate, graduating magna cum laude, from Texas Southern University, and then graduated as one of three African-American women with a law degree from Boston University in 1959. She passed the Massachusetts and Texas bars in 1960.

Jordan opened a private law practice in 1960 and later won a seat in the Texas Senate in 1966. She was re-elected to the Texas Senate in 1968 and served until 1972, when she was elected to the House of Representatives. She was the first woman elected in her own right to represent Texas in the House.

Perhaps Jordan's most memorable moment was delivering a speech before the U.S. House Judiciary Committee, supporting the impeachment of President Richard Nixon. Her eloquent and intelligent speech is often credited as the reason that Nixon resigned, recognizing that he could not defend the points that Jordan eloquently raised.

Margaret Thatcher (The Iron Lady)

Margaret Thatcher was the first female Prime Minister of the United Kingdom. She was also the longest-serving British prime minister of the twentieth century. Thatcher held office for three full terms from 1979 until 1990. She was renowned for her uncompromising leadership style and was commonly known in the press as the "Iron Lady."

Thatcher was always a controversial figure in British politics, mostly due to her hardline policies and her drive to privatize national services. Her popularity nosedived during a period of recession and high unemployment, and her financial and anti-unionist policies were frequently met with resistance from the opposition.

One of her most controversial actions was the closure of several British mines and her refusal to meet the demands of the miner's union. A year-long miners' strike ensued, and, eventually, the union conceded. During the 1980s, Thatcher was often described as the most powerful woman in the world. In 1999, Time Magazine listed her as one of the most important people of the twentieth century.

The Differences in Recognized Female Leadership Roles

While history provides a rich source of evidence that women can successfully lead, female leadership hasn't been taken seriously until more recently. One of the reasons for that is very few women rose to a leadership position in their own right. Most historical female leaders obtained their position from either privilege of birth or privilege of marriage. Often, their leadership was controversial in some way and all the more complicated because they were female.

Cleopatra had a valid claim to the Egyptian throne, but it took an alliance and an affair with a powerful man to secure her position.

When the throne was secured, she was, by most non-Western accounts around that time, a great ruler and a keen scholar and scientist. Unfortunately, her actual achievements as a leader are glossed over in historical accounts with her affairs taking center stage over her leadership skills. For the vast majority of women throughout history, the idea of them being able to hold the kind of positions that were open to men was unthinkable.

Of course, some of the historical barriers to leadership have always been class and not just purely gender. However, the fact remains that even women born into wealthy households for most of history would not have been encouraged to aspire too much beyond becoming a dutiful wife and a good mother.

In the list above, Margaret Thatcher stands out as one woman who carved out a highly successful political career on the back of her own achievements. However, it's interesting to note that her leadership style is often described in more masculine terms. More often than not, this is in a detrimental tone rather than celebratory of her strengths. She was certainly more of an autocratic leader than a laissez-faire one. It could also be argued that, at times, she demonstrated traits consistent with a transformational leader, for example, having the vision and ability to pull an entire country through a period of significant change. Factually, she left Britain financially stronger than when she found it, regardless of people's opinions on how she achieved that—something that is not often recognized and celebrated.

The Glass Ceiling

As just explored, historically, there were female leaders, but they were the outliers, anomalies, and they often faced severe opposition. In the early twentieth century, women were still not allowed to vote. And, even after gaining the vote in 1920, thanks to the work of Eleanor Roosevelt, the path of equality with leadership positions remained out of reach due to a lack of equal education opportunities.

Women were still denied access to many higher educational opportunities, such as Ivy League colleges. Getting a degree from a college like Harvard was impossible until 1963. And, without access to those opportunities, women were poorly placed to step into leadership positions.

Fortunately, present-day situations are changing, albeit too slowly. A small number (6%) of leaders in Fortune 500 companies are now women, but, until 1972, when Katherine Graham became CEO of the Washington Post, there were none (except Anna Bissell, CEO of Bissell, from 1889 until 1919). So, when did thinking start to shift from corporate leadership being a male-only occupation? Entering the 1960s, even with a good college education, women were only expected to fulfill secretarial and admin roles. Few, if any, corporations would even consider interviewing a woman for a management position or a professional role. The reasoning for this inequality was accepted social gender roles—men should be the breadwinners and women should be looking after the home and children.

It wasn't until the 1970s, that these views were challenged, and opinions began to shift slightly. It appears society forgot about the Rosy the Riveters, the countless women, mothers and daughters who went to work in the factories while their husbands and fathers were off fighting World War II. The Equal Rights movements and their influence meant women were no longer explicitly excluded from managerial roles. However, there were still limits on what they could achieve. Only lower levels of management were attainable, yet, it was a move in the right direction.

The oft-used term "glass ceiling" to describe the invisible but very real barrier preventing women from accessing higher-level leadership roles was first used by the Wall Street Journal in 1986. The concept of the glass ceiling caught on quickly, and eventually the U.S. Congress established an investigatory commission specifically for the glass ceiling idea. In their report, they noted that the glass ceiling was driven by the notion that women were likely to quit working to start a family. No executives were willing to hire women for important roles because of the possibility that they might start a family.

New laws were passed to prevent the exclusion of women from

leadership roles. As a result, over a length of time, there has been a rise in the number of female leaders in high-level positions. On a positive note for women in the present day, it is now easier than it has ever been for women to rise through the ranks of leadership.

Unfortunately, the path to higher levels of leadership for women still isn't as clear as it is for their male counterparts, but the situation is progressing at a rapid pace. It's not true that women are better leaders than men, nor is it true that men are better leaders than women. Ability and talent are determined by many things, such as upbringing, socio-economic background, genetics, education, and environment—NOT GENDER!

However, it is true that men have always been given more opportunities to lead than women have. In the next chapter, we'll look at what, if any, general differences there are between men and women when it comes to leadership. We'll also explore why there is still a lack of female leaders in the twenty-first century.

These concepts are worth exploring as fuel to validate your why and empower you to write your own story as a woman entrepreneur. For me, my frustration with the glass ceiling grew very high as an employee. It is another reason why I walk this road and choose to run my own entrepreneurial businesses.

CHAPTER FIVE – BREAKING DOWN BARRIERS

**"If you want something said, ask a man.
If you want something done, ask a woman."
- Former United Kingdom Prime Minister Margaret Thatcher**

Breaking down gender barriers doesn't just positively affect women, although, arguably it's women who stand to gain the most from a more equal society. However, gender stereotypes and roles can (and do!) have an adverse impact on men as well as women.

Let's consider for a moment the impact of gender stereotypes on men.

Men displaying traits associated with femininity can find themselves ridiculed, and men can feel just as much pressure to steer clear from careers traditionally associated with women. Men are often told that "real" men don't cry. Crying is something that women do; it is a sign of their emotional instability and a sign of weakness. Yet in reality, crying is normal human behavior for both men and women. It's also a natural and powerful way to relieve emotional stress. Discouraging men from crying leaves them bottling up emotions that they're not sure how to express for fear of being seen as weak.

The flipside of men being the dominant gender in the workforce is men often equate their worth with their career. Their worth is then derived and associated with their salary. High-earning men are considered to be powerful. In contrast, a woman's worth tends to be tied to her looks or her nurturing abilities. Women are often left frustrated when their careers stall after childbirth. However, men feel immense pressure to be a suitable breadwinner in a household that's dropped from two incomes to one. It can also lead to men feeling embarrassed and emasculated if their female partner earns a higher income.

By breaking down gender barriers, we make strides towards a more just and equal society. Will it fix all of society's issues? No, but, just like houses are built brick by brick, we need to lay the foundations of a just and equal society. Gender is one place to start. Besides the favorable reasons to promote more gender diverse leadership in workplaces, there are tangible business benefits to promoting diversity at work.

Let's examine some key benefits that businesses can expect from becoming more gender diverse. As your business builds make sure you are paying attention to this. It is easy to fall into a pattern of hiring people just like you; but, how will your business grow if everyone is a cookie cutter of you? You will miss out on the benefit of a diverse employee pool. It is always that one employee, the one who thinks differently than you, who has the innovative idea you are not thinking of, that will take your business to the next level.

Benefits of Breaking Down Gender Stereotypes

Hire and Retain the Best People

Businesses exist for one reason—to make money and be successful. Even non-profits, and yes, my fellow sister entrepreneurs need to run their businesses effectively so they can give back to others. To encourage better gender diversity, it is crucial that businesses assess their hiring and promotion processes. These two processes are the biggest factor in promoting more diversity. Yet, many companies still have hiring and promotion processes that put women at a distinct disadvantage. Unfortunately, this indirect discrimination against female candidates is also putting businesses at a distinct disadvantage.

Women make up half of the talent pool. Not only that, according to the National Center for Education Statistics, women are the most qualified half. In the 2018-2019 academic year, women will earn over 57% of all awarded bachelor's degrees and over 51% of doctorates. Women who do make it to the top of the corporate ladder tend to have more academic qualifications than their male colleagues. Yet, despite female graduates out-numbering men, women are less likely to be hired into entry-level jobs.

At management-level jobs, this gap widens even further. Female candidates are much less likely to be hired into management level jobs. They are also much less likely to be promoted into them. Overall, only 38% of all management level positions are held by women. If this doesn't change, the rate of growth in the number of women leaders is going to be painfully slow. When women are under-represented at every stage of the career ladder, there are fewer women qualified to become C-suite leaders. Yet, if companies start addressing these lower-level gaps now, that gap will close much quicker.

More choices for women also provide more candidate choices for businesses. In turn, this means that businesses can attract and retain the very best people for their organization. Creating career paths that are clearer, along with providing working opportunities that are less hostile to women, will allow women to be more motivated and driven to help the business succeed. Remember this as you build your own business leadership team.

Having a higher proportion of female leaders doesn't just lead to a better and more balanced recruitment process. It also leads to a lower staff turnover rate. Lower turnover is something that can save businesses a lot of money each year. When you're not spending large portions of your budget replacing and retraining staff that have left, you can concentrate on developing existing staff. This extra investment makes them more motivated and increases their loyalty and performance.

As I have discussed, there needs to be a focus on the bottom-up hiring processes, but there is also value in a focus on getting women into senior leadership roles. Once a business has recruited a good ratio of female leaders into its ranks, there is a trickle-down effect.

BENEFIT: Having more females positioned as senior leaders leads to less gender discrimination in recruitment, business operations and promotions.

Having a Diversity Policy Can Make You More Attractive to Potential Employees

Millennials make up the largest segment of the workforce today. Research by U.K. consultancy PwC showed that over three-quarters of female millennials consider a prospective employer's culture, their equality policy, and the company's diversity policy. In fact, 61% of women overall take into account the gender diversity of a prospective employer's leadership when deciding where to work. By not having policies that promote diversity, you are potentially losing out on being an attractive employment prospect for some of the best talent.

It is important to note that a good hiring process doesn't mean favoring female candidates. It simply means that the process should encourage all candidates and allow the hiring manager to select the best person for the role. With that in mind, can any business really afford to discourage or ignore the most academically qualified half of the population when it comes to hiring?

BENEFIT: Having a well written and socialized diversity policy makes you attractive to the best female talent.

Higher Employee Engagement and Performance

It's a well-documented fact that employees who are more engaged with their organization are more productive, take fewer sick days, and are better employees all around. As a result, most organizations place employee engagement high on their priority list. Top business leaders understand that a high-performing workforce is essential for the growth of the business. The problem they face is how to achieve higher employee engagement.

Regular surveys of employees give an indication of what can be improved and what is often overlooked. Surveys are powerful and contribute greatly to creating a diverse and engaged workforce. A lot of gender bias is unconscious and generally unintended - but that doesn't make it less harmful. When these biases go unnoticed, even by other women, it leaves workers with a sense of unease. We know something isn't right, and that we want something more from the organization's policies. Unfortunately, we aren't sure how to ask for it or even sometimes, how to identify the problem. We don't feel fully engaged with the business, but we don't know how to explain why.

Employee surveys have their place but results often show that people want more pay (not always possible across the board) and benefits. This results in employers introducing perks like free coffee, casual Fridays, or employee competitions. These gimmicky solutions have a small place in engagement, but they don't tend to drive real and sustainable engagement.

Studies have shown that a working environment that promotes diversity makes employees feel respected, engaged, and involved with the business at a greater level. When this happens, employees are more productive and invested in their roles. In turn, customers and clients receive better service.

BENEFIT: Employees who are more engaged with their organization are more productive, take fewer sick days, and are better employees all around.

Promote Creativity

Diversity also encourages collaboration, creativity, and problem-solving, meaning you get more out of your employees. When diverse groups collaborate, the combination of unique perspectives leads to better ideas. Further, that feeling of inclusivity trickles down to your clients and customers making them more loyal to your brand.

In an interview with CNBC, Joe Carella, the Assistant Dean of the University of Arizona, Eller College of Management, confirmed that gender-diverse companies do become more creative. He said, "We did our own analysis of Fortune 500 companies, and we found that companies that have women in top management roles experience what we call 'innovation intensity' and produce more patents - by an average of 20 percent more than teams with male leaders."

There is a lot of research demonstrating that diverse teams develop more innovative ideas. A diverse leadership team is more likely to promote an environment where ideas are shared, and creative ideas are considered. It is potentially down to the link between diversity and transformational leadership - which is also shown to encourage creative thinking. However, to gain these benefits, your business needs to truly support and promote diversity. In order to contribute freely to discussions and generate innovative ideas and solutions, people need to feel safe and valued. If people don't feel safe to share their ideas, or that their ideas are not valued by their peers and line management, they will simply stop contributing. It's not enough to just place more women in leadership positions. They need to feel safe and encouraged to contribute. When that happens, the boost to creativity can be remarkable.

BENEFIT: When diverse groups are free to collaborate, the combination of unique perspectives leads to better ideas.

Drive Business Profits and Performance

Having a gender-diverse business directly relates to having a more successful business. If business owners have been wondering why they should bother encouraging diversity, then this is potentially the most compelling reason. If you're running a business, a healthier bottom line is always your key objective.

In fact, a McKinsey & Company report calculated that increasing gender diversity in the workplace could add $12 trillion to the global economy. Further research by McKinsey & Company demonstrated that businesses with a healthy balance of men and women are 15% more likely to outperform their competitors. Clearly, the reasons for businesses to take gender diversity seriously are about more than just fairness and equality. Gender diversity isn't just a tick in the politically correct box; it is a competitive financial strategy.

Not convinced? A five-year study conducted by MSCI Inc. into the performance of companies in the U.S.A. had some interesting insights. Between 2011 and 2016, they found that businesses with a minimum of three women on the board had 45% higher earnings per share compared to those with none. A further Gallup study across two industries investigated over 800 business units. They discovered that gender-diverse business units generated an average of 14% more revenue and a 19% higher quarterly net profit than those with less diversity.

In yet another study, Harvard Kennedy School investigated employee gender in relation to sales and profits. They demonstrated that teams with an equal gender mix perform better than male-dominated teams in terms of sales and profits. They noted that sales and profits continued to increase proportionately in relation to the percentage of women, up to 50%. For teams with a higher proportion of women, there wasn't a decrease in performance compared to teams who were mostly male. However, they performed around the same level as the teams with an equal gender mix. What is especially interesting here is that the study looked at the performance of sales teams—which are typically male-dominated.

The relationship between high-performing companies and companies with a high percentage of female leaders is eye-opening. Research by the Peterson Institute for International Economics demonstrated that there is a correlation between higher profits and the number of women in the C-Suite. Companies with 30% or more of their leadership positions filled by women had at least a 1% higher net profit margin when compared to companies without female leaders. The amount of research demonstrating the relationship between a diverse leadership team and higher profit is staggering.

So, why do the more diverse businesses perform better? It is not necessarily true that women are better leaders but having more diversity at the decision-making level helps businesses perform better. In-group bias or "group-think" hurts a company's bottom-line. It is demonstrated repeatedly that cultural diversity, as well as gender diversity, improves performance overall.

Without diversity at a senior level, a poor retention rate and disengaged employees could be the least of your issues. Shortly after the financial crisis, Sallie Krawcheck, co-founder and CEO of Ellevest and a former executive at Morgan Stanley and Citibank, blamed Wall Street's issue with "groupthink" for contributing to the crisis. In an interview with CBS, she said, "There was no doubt that had we had more diversity of thought, perspective, education, gender, color, the crisis would have been less severe." She might have a point. In fact, after Iceland's banking crisis, the only bank left standing was headed by female leaders.

BENEFIT: Diversity leads to a healthier bottom line and increased profit.

Attract Investors

In the same way that having a gender-diverse workforce and robust diversity policies can help you attract the best talent; they can also help you attract good investors for your business or non-profit. Several studies have highlighted that companies who adopt best practice policies, like a hiring process that encourages diversity, are seen as more attractive to investors. There is even research to suggest that when a business wins an award related to diversity, their stock prices increase.

However, there are caveats to this. An analysis of the research demonstrates that the industry context plays a large part in how much diversity affects investors. For industries that are traditionally male-dominated and less diverse culturally, the effect is diminished. For industries that are more aware of the benefits of promoting and keeping diversity, the effect is increased.

Having a gender-diverse workforce can positively impact how investors view the business and, it is highly unlikely to have any negative impact. As such, for businesses that haven't already done so, it makes excellent business sense to implement diversity policies as soon as possible.

BENEFIT: Diversity policies can help attract good investors for your business or non-profit.

BE SURE TO HAVE A GOOD DIVERSITY POLICY for your entrepreneurial business. Visit the Federal Government's Office of

Personal Management to see an example of a Diversity Policy - https://www.opm.gov/policy-data-oversight/diversity-and-inclusion.

Real Life Case Study – James

James is the CEO of a large marketing consultancy. While his company continually made a profit, the level of profit had been stagnant year after year. Understandably, James wanted to drive the business to higher levels of success. When his HR director presented him with a report citing research from Credit Suisse demonstrating an 18% return-on-investment premium for gender-diverse leadership teams, James knew he needed to pay attention.

Working closely with his HR team, James laid out his goals to achieving gender diversity in the business. His first goal, over the next five years, 30% of the leadership in the C-suite will be female. His second goal, to have at least 40% of all employees in each department be female.

To discover the best way to get achieve these goals, James held a meeting with all his current female employees to understand what barriers they faced and how to remove them. His meeting uncovered that his female employees felt that the culture of long working hours was holding them back. Even if they produced the same amount and quality of work as employees who worked longer hours, his employees with caring responsibilities felt overlooked for recognition and promotion opportunities.

Further, James uncovered a prevailing sense among female employees that the C-suite would be an unwelcoming environment for a female. When James asked why they felt that way, they mentioned that there was only one female leader out of nine board members. James's first step was introducing a reward and recognition scheme that rewarded employees for high-quality work rather than excessive working hours. This immediate change addressed some of his employee's concerns about how the company valued employees with caring responsibilities.

His next step was to overhaul the hiring and promotion processes. Alongside his HR team, James reviewed the end to end process, from guidelines for placing an advertisement, to how candidates were shortlisted for interviews. James took a radical approach. He suggested that all candidates who met the academic qualifications and experience criteria are entered into a database. Via this database, the hiring managers could see the person's experience and qualifications, but could not view the applicant's name, age, or gender. Based on this information, managers could select the candidates for the HR team to interview.

By removing obvious identifiers of age or gender, James was removing a potential barrier for progressing female applicants. Each applicant could be judged on their qualifications alone, making it more likely that a fair and diverse mix of candidates would be invited to interview.

Besides this radical change, they also removed any unnecessary insistence on inflexible working schedules. They published their commitment to gender diversity on their corporate website and at the bottom of any literature relating to their hiring and promotions process.

The changes James implemented took over twelve months in total to embed and to begin to make a real difference. Over a 24-month period, the business saw a 10% increase of female employees at all levels and a 16% increase in the number of women promoted to a management level position. Over the same 24-month period, net profits rose by 4%, with projections for the following year being a 6% increase.

CHAPTER SIX – THE RIGHT MINDSET AS A WOMAN ENTREPRENEUR

**"A woman is like a tea bag.
You cannot tell how strong she is until
you put her in hot water."
- Former First Lady Nancy Reagan**

This chapter is a crash course on additional skills, mindsets, and the knowledge needed to start and run a successful business. Each of the topics covered is broad and could easily be featured in their own separate book. These brief introductions are provided as a guide for you to decide what you might want to research next.

So, do you own your business, or does your business own you? Have you built a business or a job for yourself? If you don't show up for work at your business tomorrow morning, will your business continue to thrive and grow, or will it grind to a halt? What would happen if you took an unexpected week off? or a month? or a quarter?

Becoming an entrepreneur is a process that takes time, so it's important to not rush it. Learn all you can and allow yourself to enjoy the process of becoming more knowledgeable. You may face some tough times on the way, but you will also identify opportunities that could open new doors. The advantages of entrepreneurship are many. Here are a few that are the most important for me.

Freedom: Time for What You Enjoy

One of the primary advantages of being a woman entrepreneur is having freedom, the freedom of time to spend time with family and/or friends. I think time is the most precious thing in life, more important than money, which is why enjoying or spending your time the way you prefer is the greatest advantage you have as an efficient woman entrepreneur.

Control of Your Path

As a woman entrepreneur, you will be able to make most of your own decisions. You'll make some mistakes, but you'll learn from them. So, with time and practice, you'll become more confident in yourself and more in control of your path, which will result in a better future. As a woman entrepreneur, the decision and control joystick are in your hands. Having that kind of control is a remarkably great feeling, and it will allow you to turn the impossible into possible if you know how to dream big and take consistent actions to make your dreams reality.

Acquiring Authority and Recognition

An entrepreneur is a leader rather than a follower. This puts you in a position of earning recognition from other people, appearing unique because you are the inventor, founder, and creator of your dream product or service - perhaps a project, or a company, or maybe a movement to save people in Africa. Being a follower is not a bad thing. We are all followers at one time or another, and we need to learn to be good followers to become good leaders. But leaders have a greater impact on people and on the world. Now is your time to build better ideas, provide more value to others, and inspire everyone around you.

Building a Stronger Network

Networking with more people at different levels is another advantage of entrepreneurship. You will meet many other people from different companies, and likely network inside and outside your company; how often and how much depends on the size and quality of your network, the events you attend, and the companies you target.

Some employees have larger networks than entrepreneurs, but, in general, and with the nature of the entrepreneurial life, entrepreneurs not only have a more expansive network than employees, but they tend to network at a higher and more targeted level, using such connections to open many doors for future business deals, partnerships, financing, and different investment opportunities.

Adding Value through Innovation

When you are in the process of inventing a new product or a new service you must think about - how is my new "xyz" thing going to add value to other people. Helping others by adding value will make you successful. When you add value, the money will follow.

Laying the Path to Independence

Being an entrepreneur gives you independence - it gives you the confidence to make your own decisions and to be in control of your own path, as it is shaped by your own decisions.

The Woman Entrepreneur Mindset and Focus

One thing I have learned on my own entrepreneurial journey is that good things are very rarely accomplished all by yourself. In fact, success (more often than not) hinges on receiving the best advice and support from the people who really do know. At some stage, we all have mentors in our lives, whether we realize it or not. Below are some of the mindsets that women entrepreneurs should have in order to achieve success.

Giving Up Is Not an Option

Millionaires and billionaires continue with the growth mindset that helps them get to where they want to be. They are completely goal centered and focused on achieving their vision. They (absolutely) will not give up until they achieve them. Perseverance and sustainable effort are always the key here.

Take Complete Responsibility

Experiencing setbacks is part of the journey, and, psychologically, women entrepreneurs need to know that it is just a hiccup or an inconvenient speed bump in a much bigger plan - a well-thought-out plan that will ultimately come to fruition through hard work and perseverance. Losing sight of your end goal should never be an option.

Take Some Risks

Women entrepreneurs play the wealth game to win. They should allow opportunities to be utilized, with a mindset of not losing what they have. Sometimes, taking a gamble will pay off, and sometimes it won't. But failure, remember, is just a steppingstone. They see it as a learning curve that can and will be pushed through.

Build Your Business through Networking

Many entrepreneurs speak of the importance of networking. However, few explain why networking is of such extreme significance because they are so laser focused on doing it!

First of all, it is crucial to measure the return on investment you will get from any networking efforts. Be intentional about who you are networking with. We become the sum of those we associate with.

Second, something of value must be given first when making initial connections, rather than asking for something in the beginning.

Third, always be ready to accept a pearl of wisdom.

Fourth, be ready to help another soul on their journey. Instead of seeing your entrepreneurial sister as a competitor figure out how you can partner together.

Fifth, never assume someone is disposable based on their appearance. Some woman you see in rags could be a wealthy dowager looking for a genuine soul to invest in. If you desire to learn more about networking, I suggest the book "Never Eat Alone," by Keith Ferazzi or "How to Win Friends & Influence People," by Dale Carnegie.

CHAPTER SEVEN – MAKING IT AS AN ENTREPRENEUR

"Everyone has inside of her a piece of good news. The good news is that you don't know how great you can be, how much you can love, what you can accomplish, and what your potential is."
- Anne Frank

Motivation

There are two kinds of motivation: intrinsic and extrinsic. Intrinsic motivation comes from inside you. It is an inner drive you feel when you are excited about something and doing what you love. This is usually a long-term motivation toward something. It is that strong inner drive that the great entrepreneurship authors wrote about.

Typically, extrinsic motivation is short-term. A motivation you might get from something external like an energetic song, motivational pep talk, or a reward for yourself, such as a fun trip or a new pair of shoes, the motivational effects of which dissipate within minutes, hours, or days.

While both types of motivation are useful, intrinsic motivation is much more helpful to encourage you over the lifetime of your business. If you are working on well-chosen goals and have put your life trajectory on a path that is right for you, much of your motivation will naturally be intrinsic.

On the other hand, if you have mistakenly chosen the wrong goals, given into external pressures, and are not working on the things that excite you, you will be naturally less motivated, which will lead to lower interest in your work and lower quality of execution, followed by low confidence. Lack of motivation, inadequate execution, or low confidence can be a signal that you selected a goal that doesn't excite you. It all starts with getting to know yourself better and becoming more self-aware, so you understand what is right for YOU to pursue.

Dramatic Productivity Boost

Whenever top CEOs are surveyed about how they approach productivity, they often answer that they do less work. They identify less fruitful tasks and simply remove those from their schedule. For example, out of ten things you have on your to-do list right now, probably two or three will pay the highest dividends and the others will be much less effective toward getting you closer to your goals. The trick is to identify the tasks on your to-do list with the most and least potential and remove the low-potential tasks. You may immediately gain more time to work on the high-potential tasks, which will allow you to execute those tasks better, making them even more beneficial.

Delegation, Outsourcing, and Automation

Keep an eye out for inefficient processes in your business and consider whether they could be fixed by doing them differently, hiring outside help, finding software to expedite them, or even having custom software built for you.

If you are just starting and don't have a big budget for outsourcing or building software, start with a budget as low as $50 per month. That isn't a lot to spend, but you might be surprised by how many extra tasks you can get done if you outsource carefully and intelligently by hiring freelancers on websites like Fiverr.com or UpWork.com. Plus, this will give you practice outsourcing and automating for when your business grows, and you have a bigger budget.

Mitigating Risk

There are three somewhat different types of risks you face when starting a business:
1. Product risk
2. Market risk
3. Financial risk

Not all businesses have each of these risks. As you move through this section, think about which risks apply to your situation.

Product risk arises when your product is too expensive, complicated, or difficult to produce, which could prevent it from ever being created. If you can't build your product, you will never launch it. Even if you're able to produce your product initially, it may be too expensive or complicated to evolve and improve the product due to the costs that come with complexity.

The second type of risk is market risk. This is the danger that once you launch your product, customers won't buy it and sales will be slow or nonexistent. Innovative products typically have significant market risk. A cleaning business or a lawn care business have minimal market risk, because such services have a natural demand.

The third type of risk is financial risk. Some businesses have minimal financial risk, and some have quite a bit of risk. You must know your tolerance for risking your money and make sure not to choose a business that requires more money than you are prepared to risk.

Avoid Procrastination

People procrastinate for different reasons. For most people, procrastination is a habit. A habit is a learned behavior that can be stopped if you form a new healthier habit to replace the old habit. Studies show that it takes about three weeks of daily behavior to form a new habit. You must force yourself to do things in a new way, and, after a few weeks, you will no longer need to force yourself. You will just do the new, healthier behavior naturally without thinking about it. The hardest part of breaking your procrastination habit is taking the first steps to reverse your previously learned behavior, replacing it with another, and not relapsing later.

Reversing the NO Mentality

Many entrepreneurs often say things like "if I only had money to start my business," or "I'll wait until I have more free time in three months," or "I don't have an engineer to build my product so I won't start," and many other similar statements. Having this mentality prevents people from starting their businesses. Entrepreneurs find solutions to problems. Want-a-be-entrepreneurs find excuses, feel sorry for themselves, blame external forces, and let problems derail their efforts.

If you find yourself not starting until some barrier goes away, try to change your mindset or your launch strategy. You must be resourceful and creative to find solutions to problems. There will always be roadblocks and problems. Problems are a part of the entrepreneur experience, and new ones will arise every day. Embrace them and learn to solve them.

Keep in mind that there are often many possible solutions to one problem, and you should try to discover better ways to solve your problems instead of allowing barriers to halt your progress. If you are struggling in this area, find an accountability partner. Set check-in meetings on a regular basis such as weekly. Find someone who can stick their thumb in your back and motivate you to act.

Your Ego

As you start your business, and especially if you manage to grow it, many people will praise you and tell you how smart and accomplished you are. As success accelerates, so does praise. As entrepreneurs, we start to believe it.

Don't.

Stay humble!

What you are doing might be great, but there is always more to learn and ways to improve. This is a much healthier mindset. If you let your ego become too large, you will convince yourself that you are great the way you are, you don't need to improve anymore, and that will be the beginning of the end. Instead, keep the attitude that you are always just at the relative beginning and you need to learn more and improve in many ways.

Additionally, your feeling of self-worth should come from within instead of from the empty praise of others. You will get a lot of praise if you are in the 90th percentile in your field. But you can't rest there. There is still a long way to go until you reach the 99th percentile.

Dealing with Stress

Starting my business was one of the most stressful periods of my life. There was stress from lack of finances, business uncertainty, pressure from family and friends, self-doubt, etc. My greatest stress came from me believing things were not moving fast enough. I wanted to be out of my 9-5, time-stealing, freedom snatching job, as they say, yesterday. It almost stole my joy in the journey. If you are in the process of starting your business now, believe me, I understand what you're going through. Not only did I go through the same stressful period in my life, but I coach many people who are in your exact situation.

Among the many negative things resulting from stress, one especially damaging byproduct for your business is that it forces you to make short-term decisions aimed at making a quick buck in the hope to relieve the stress. This comes at the expense of long-term planning that can set you up for much greater success.

Remember the saying "haste makes waste." When you start your business, haste is often forced by stress and the seeking of immediate benefits, and haste usually creates a lot of waste. Be careful of stress having too much influence over your business decisions.

Dealing with Failure

Albert Einstein once said

> "Anyone who has never made a mistake has never
> tried anything new."

As soon as you step out of your comfort zone, you will begin to fail. See it as a good sign instead of a bad one. Every failure or criticism is either a sign that you're learning or a clue to what you can improve. You can use those clues to unearth blind spots in your business and fix them.

When Thomas Edison was asked how it felt to fail 10,000 times when working on the filament for the light bulb, he responded,

> "I have not failed. I've just found 10,000 ways that won't work."

That's the attitude you must take. To take it a step further, how can you turn a perceived failure into an opportunity? Let me share a personal experience. I was invited to be one of many featured speakers at an event to promote my business and network. Well, the other speakers before me talked WAY to long and people began to leave. By the time I had the floor everyone had left or was leaving. I was very discouraged.

I woke up the next day and asked myself, "How can I turn this into an opportunity?" I did meet some wonderful ladies and we exchanged business cards. I crafted a well worded email to the few contacts I made, explaining who I was and what my business does. I invited them to join my mailing list on my website and a few of the ladies did. One of them became a client.

It is much easier to accept failure or criticism if you don't let your ego become too big. Enlarged egos tend to cause fear of failure, which leads to stagnation, lack of innovation, and indecision.

When someone criticizes any of my songs or posts negative reviews on a video, it doesn't feel good. But, deep down, I know that their opinion could be shared by others, and if I listen to them closely, they can give me hints for how I can improve my products. We can even come to appreciate our critics for caring enough to take the time to voice their concerns.

Of course, it shouldn't be all about negative reviews. For example, if you find the book helpful, I'd appreciate a positive review on Amazon.

At the same time, people can flat out be unkind and mean. Take it with a grain of salt and don't let it rattle you or derail your success. Don't become so fixated on the negative noise because it can cause you lose productivity in your business.

Embracing Work

Business can sound exciting, but under all the glamour (is there really any glamour in it?) there is boring and hard work. It's fun to plan, strategize, and dream about your business, but that does not represent the day-to-day work on your business. The day-to-day work contains hard and often monotonous work. Many people hesitate at the prospect of hard work; but if you embrace it, you will give yourself a chance to be much more successful long-term.

Visualizing Success

While it's important to do more work than dream about your business, visualizing your success can be very helpful. Daydreaming about your success and visualizing success can help you see yourself after having achieved your business goals, and cement that reality in your mind, helping you believe that you can achieve it.

Just like athletes visualize themselves crossing the finish line of a race, remember, that is how we started - with my 5K race - you must visualize yourself being successful. That vision will give you a target to work toward which will draw you to success like a magnet. Plus, it's fun to daydream.

CONCLUSION AND CHOICES

"We need women at all levels, including the top, to change the dynamic, reshape the conversation, to make sure women's voices are heard and heeded, not overlooked and ignored."
- Sheryl Sandberg

Here are a few final words of encouragement for you.

1. Ditch Perfectionism

Stop comparing yourself, stop trying to uphold an unrealistic image of yourself. Aim high but accept that failure and setbacks are part of life for everybody. With an assertive, positive mindset, you will begin to look at these as opportunities to learn from and improve. Letting go of perfectionism allows you to take more action, get more done, and potentially make more progress in your career. Good and done beats perfect every time.

2. Create Time to Grow and Nurture Yourself

It is important to take time out for your self-development and self-care. What that looks like can be different for every individual, but the key is to create the time, protect it, and use it in the best possible way. It might be reading a book; it might be taking time to reflect, time for planning, or time setting personal development goals for yourself.

It might be a spa day. It could be time to complete online courses or time to attend a night class. Do whatever energizes you and helps you grow as a leader.

Embrace the businesswoman trait in you by starting the business you have been dreaming about since you were a little girl. No more procrastination! Get that website live and sell your product or service.

3. Embrace Who You Are

We know that simply behaving like a man doesn't usually work for a woman. While there are certain lessons we can learn from the way men tend to do things, such as being more confident and being less of a perfectionist, behaving in a way that feels unnatural will come across as false to others and might even make you unhappy. Allow yourself to express your opinions and handle situations in a way that makes the best use of your strengths, instead of trying to fit into a mold made for someone else.

In conclusion, I wrote this book to empower women entrepreneurs. Within its pages, we've looked at how women have been held back in the workplace. We've looked at the tenacity of just a few of the many, amazing women who are exemplary leaders.

My challenge to you is simple, **"Go, be extraordinary**, and kick-start your business."** Reach your potential by learning from other leading ladies. Embrace the mindset needed to lead your entrepreneurial business like a boss. Like me, the 9-5 glass ceiling could be one of the reasons you're on the entrepreneur's path.

Whatever the reason is, the very fact that you're reading a book to help you start or to do what you do better, proves you got what it takes!

"You have to have confidence in your ability, and then be tough enough to follow through" - Rosalynn Carter

ABOUT THE AUTHOR

"The only way to survive is to create opportunity, rather than to wait for it to come to you"
- Judith LeComte Baker

Judith Baker, MBA, MIT created LeBaker Music to do what she loves: empowering and helping others by combining her skills in leadership and music. Owned and operated by this award-winning and well-respected servant leader, the company was birthed from years of expertise and education in music, leadership, and training.

As a natural born encourager and life learner, she began her studies as a music major. Now, Judith holds an undergraduate degree in Business and Environmental Management from the University of Phoenix and a master's degree in Business Administration and Information Technology from Bethel University. In information technology, she holds certifications in Agile, ITIL Foundations, & ITIL Service Design Engineering; and she holds a diploma in Project Management.

As a certified John Maxwell Leadership Speaker, Trainer and Coach, highly skilled at speaking, training, leading masterminds and lunch-in-learns - both in person or virtually, she enjoys helping her clients find solutions. Musically, and as of the date of this publication, she has performed in 30 states, on 38 military installations, and in 5 countries. Her first solo public appearance occurred at the age of 4 and she wrote her first original song at age 14. A gifted singer, songwriter, actress and model she is also a military Veteran that is no stranger to her audience from the podium or platform.

Above all, as an entrepreneurial minded strategic leader, Judith created her baby - "LeBaker Music" (a combination of her maiden and married surnames). This is who she is and what she loves. LeBaker Music is all about combining the forces of music and leadership to create an experience instead of another lecture. In addition to leadership training and speaking events LeBaker music, also creates custom original songs, and music for film & TV.

Some of her clients include: Asurion, the U.S. Army, the State of TN, the Medical University of South Carolina, North Charleston Sewer District (SC), The Church of the Nazarene, Trevecca Nazarene University, Boise State University (ID), The Fort Stewart (GA) Women's Association, The National Safety Council, the American Red Cross, Stonecroft Ministries, A Soldiers Child Foundation, and numerous churches and corporate events. Learn more about Judith at LeBakerMusic.com/judith-baker-bio

* * *

Thank you for reading my book. If you enjoyed it, won't you please take a moment to leave me a review at your favorite retailer? Thanks!

You can connect with me at ...

Ways to Subscribe
Subscribe to my blog: https:/lebakermusic.com/blog

Subscribe to my YouTube Channel:
https:/www.youtube.com/channel/UCod1DB9kD4ZkgH4TBer1OuQ

Website
LeBakerMusic.com

Social Media Sites
- LinkedIn: linkedin.com/in/isingit2
- Facebook Page: facebook.com/LeBakerMusic
- Instagram: instagram.com/LeBakerMusic

For more books written by Judith visit her Amazon Author Page

www.ingramcontent.com/pod-product-compliance
Lightning Source LLC
Chambersburg PA
CBHW030522220526
45463CB00007B/2674